Moon Surname

Ireland: 1600s to 1900s

From Ireland Church Records of Baptism, Marriage and Death

Comprised of Roman Catholic and Church of Ireland Records

From Counties Carlow, Cork, Kerry and Dublin City

Compiled by **Donovan Hurst**

February 20, 2013

Dedication

This work is dedicated to all of those that came before us and shaped our lives to make us the people that we are today.

Table of Contents

Introduction

This is a compilation of individuals who have the surname of Moon that lived in the country of Ireland from the 1600s to the 1900s. I have placed each entry into one of four categories: Families, Individual Births/Baptisms, Individual Burials, and Individual Marriages. If a marriage entry primarily concerns an Individual Moon whom is female, then I have placed that entry under the category of Individual Marriages. If a marriage entry primarily concerns an Individual Moon whom is male, then I have placed that entry under the category of Families. Images of many of these listings are available at http://churchrecords.irishgenealogy.ie/churchrecords/.

To help guide the reader of this work, the format of this book is as follows:

- Main Family Entry (Husband and Wife) (Father and Mother)

  - Child of Main Family Entry, including Spouse(s) when available

    - Grandchild of Main Family Entry, including Spouse(s) when available

    - Great-Grandchild of Main Family Entry, including Spouse(s) when available

(**Bolded Text**) following any entry includes any additional information such as Residence(s), Occupation(s), Signature(s), etc. when available.

Hurst

Some of the fonts used in this work symbolizes Celtic writing. The traditional letters, numbers, and punctuation marks and their Celtic counterparts are as follows:

Traditional Letters (Uppercase & Lowercase)

A a B b C c D d E f G g H h I i J j K k L l M m N n O o P p Q q R r S s T t U u V v W w X x Y y Z z

Celtic Letters (Uppercase & Lowercase)

A a B b C c D ð E e F f G g H h I i J j K k L l M m

N n O o P p Q q R r S s T t U u V v W w X x Y y Z z

Traditional Numbers

1 2 3 4 5 6 7 8 9 10

Celtic Numbers

1 2 3 4 5 6 7 8 9 10

Traditional Punctuation

. , : ' " & - ( )

Celtic Punctuation

. , : ' " & - ( )

Moon Surname Ireland: 1600s to 1900s

Parish Churches

Carlow (Church of Ireland)

Aghold Parish.

Cork & Ross

(Roman Catholic or RC)

Caharagh Parish, Clonakilty Parish, Cork - South Parish, SS. Peter & Paul Parish, Kinsale Parish, and Rossalettiri & Kilkeraunmor (Roscarbery & Lissevard) Parish.

Dublin (Church of Ireland)

Arbour Hill Barracks Parish, Clontarf Parish, Glasnevin Parish, Leeson Park Parish, St. Audoen Parish, St. Catherine Parish, St. George Parish, St. James Parish, St. John Parish, St. Mark Parish, St. Mary Parish, St. Michan Parish, St. Nicholas Within Parish, St. Nicholas Without Parish, St. Paul Parish, St. Peter Parish, and Taney Parish.

Dublin (Roman Catholic or RC)

Chapelizod Parish, Harrington Street Parish, Rathmines Parish, SS. Michael & John Parish, St. Agatha Parish, St. Andrew Parish, St. Audoen Parish, St. Catherine Parish, St. James Parish, St. Lawrence Parish, St. Mary Parish, St. Mary, Pro Cathedral Parish, St. Michan Parish, and St. Nicholas Parish.

Kerry (Church of Ireland)

Tralee Parish.

Kerry (Roman Catholic or RC)

Abbeydorney Parish, and Ballyferriter Parish.

Families

- Alfred Moon & Ellen Donnelly

  o Eileen Honor Moon – b. 10 Oct 1895, bapt. 15 Oct 1895 (Baptism, **Harrington Street Parish (RC)**)

  o Christopher Moon – b. 3 Nov 1900, bapt. 13 Nov 1900 (Baptism, **Harrington Street Parish (RC)**)

  o Emily Mary Moon – b. 14 Jul 1903, bapt. 19 Jul 1903 (Baptism, **Rathmines Parish (RC)**)

Alfred Moon (father):

Residence - 35 Victoria Street - October 15, 1895

13 Upper Clanbrassil Street - November 13, 1900

8 Le Viers Terrace, Harold's Cross - July 19, 1903

- Ambrose Moon & Charlotte Unknown

  o Ambrose Moon – bapt. 1788 (Baptism, **St. Andrew Parish (RC)**)

- Bartholomew Moon & Susan Unknown

  o John Moon – bapt. 6 Nov 1777 (Baptism, **St. Mary, Pro Cathedral Parish (RC)**)

- Charles Moon & Mary Bolger

  o Margaret Moon – b. 22 Jul 1878, bapt. 30 Jul 1878 (Baptism, **St. James Parish (RC)**)

Charles Moon (father):

Residence - Inchicore - July 30, 1878

Hurst

- Charles Moon & Monica Unknown

  o Terence Moon – bapt. 19 May 1776 (Baptism, **St. Mary, Pro Cathedral Parish (RC)**)

- Charles Moon & Sarah Mary Moon

  o William Joseph Moon – b. 29 Jul 1882, bapt. 11 Nov 1884 (Baptism, **Arbour Hill Barracks Parish**)

  o Mabel Louise Moon – b. 8 Dec 1885, bapt. 7 Mar 1888 (Baptism, **Arbour Hill Barracks Parish**)

  o Amy Elizabeth Moon – b. 19 Nov 1887, bapt. 7 Mar 1888 (Baptism, **Arbour Hill Barracks Parish**)

Charles Moon (father):

Residence - Warder's Quarters, Arbour Hill Barracks - November 11, 1884

March 7, 1888

Occupation - Warder, Military Prison - November 11, 1884

March 7, 1888

- Christopher Moon & Ellen Doran

  o Catherine Moon – bapt. 1825 (Baptism, **St. Andrew Parish (RC)**)

  o Mary Moon – bapt. 1826 (Baptism, **St. Andrew Parish (RC)**)

  o Catherine Moon – bapt. 1830 (Baptism, **St. Andrew Parish (RC)**)

  o Ellen Moon – bapt. 1835 (Baptism, **St. Andrew Parish (RC)**)

  o Ellen Moon – bapt. 6 Nov 1838 (Baptism, **St. Catherine Parish (RC)**)

  o Anne Moon – bapt. 20 May 1842 (Baptism, **St. Catherine Parish (RC)**)

Moon Surname Ireland: 1600s to 1900s

- Daniel Moon & Elizabeth Cole – 6 May 1875 (Marriage, **SS. Peter & Paul Parish (RC)**)

Daniel Moon (husband):

    Residence - 14 Kyle Street - May 6, 1875

Elizabeth Cole (wife):

    Residence - 11 Peter Church Lane - May 6, 1875

- Daniel Moon & Unknown
  - Richard Moon – bapt. 10 May 1701 (Baptism, **St. Catherine Parish**)

- Edmund Moon & Mary Connor
  - Ellen Moon – b. 22 Jan 1812, bapt. 22 Jan 1812 (Baptism, **Ballyferriter Parish (RC)**)

Edmund Moon (father):

    Residence - Balyickeen - January 22, 1812

- Edward Moon & Margaret Unknown
  - Hanes Moon – bapt. 23 Feb 1766 (Baptism, **St. James Parish**)

Edward Moon (father):

    Residence - Kilmainham - February 23, 1766

- George Moon & Eleanor Howard
  - Dennis Moon – bapt. 1799 (Baptism, **St. Mary Parish (RC)**)

- George Moon & Honor Murphy
  - Joseph Moon – bapt. 24 Feb 1844 (Baptism, **Cork - South Parish (RC)**)

- Gulielmo Moon & Elizabeth Unknown
  - Elizabeth Moon – bapt. 1822 (Baptism, **St. Andrew Parish (RC)**)

Hurst

- Henry Moon & Bridget Fay

  - Mary Moon – bapt. 1777 (Baptism, **SS. Michael & John Parish** (RC))

  - John Moon – bapt. 1778 (Baptism, **SS. Michael & John Parish** (RC))

  - Bridget Moon – bapt. 1780 (Baptism, **SS. Michael & John Parish** (RC))

  - James Moon – bapt. 1782 (Baptism, **SS. Michael & John Parish** (RC))

  - Joseph Moon – bapt. 1783 (Baptism, **SS. Michael & John Parish** (RC))

- Henry Moon & Bridget Unknown

  - Mary Moon – b. 1706, bapt. 1706 (Baptism, **SS. Michael & John Parish** (RC))

- Henry Moon & Bridget Unknown

  - John Moon – bapt. 20 Oct 1788 (Baptism, **St. Audoen Parish** (RC))

  - Peter Moon – bapt. 29 Jun 1790 (Baptism, **St. Audoen Parish** (RC))

  - David Moon – bapt. 23 Oct 1791 (Baptism, **St. Audoen Parish** (RC))

  - Mary Moon – bapt. 11 May 1794 (Baptism, **St. Audoen Parish** (RC))

- Henry Moon & Hannah Unknown

  - Hannah Moon – bapt. 15 Sep 1835 (Baptism, **St. Mary, Pro Cathedral Parish** (RC))

- Henry Moon & Honor Horan

  - Anne Lucy Moon – bapt. 28 May 1852 (Baptism, **St. Nicholas Parish** (RC))

  - Unknown Moon – b. 25 Apr 1857, bapt. 6 May 1857 (Baptism, **St. Nicholas Parish** (RC))

  - Mary Jane Moon, b. 16 Aug 1859, bapt. 22 Aug 1859 (Baptism, **St. Nicholas Parish** (RC)) & Peter Reilly – 4 Sep 1883 (Marriage, **Harrington Street Parish** (RC))

Mary Jane Moon (daughter):

Residence - 85 Hetybury Street - September 4, 1883

Moon Surname Ireland: 1600s to 1900s

Peter Reilly, son of Patrick Reilly & Margaret O'Connell (son-in-law):

Residence - 149 Great Brunswick Street - September 4, 1883

- ○ Patrick Michael Moon – b. 24 Jan 1862, bapt. 31 Jan 1862 (Baptism, **St. Nicholas Parish (RC)**)
- ○ Alfred Joseph Moon – b. 24 Jan 1868, bapt. 31 Jan 1868 (Baptism, **St. Nicholas Parish (RC)**)

Henry Moon (father):

Residence - 97 Bride Street - May 6, 1857

August 22, 1859

January 31, 1862

January 31, 1868

- Henry Moon & Lily Moon
  - ○ Lily Elizabeth Moon – b. 18 Nov 1887, bapt. 9 Dec 1887 (Baptism, **Arbour Hill Barracks Parish**)

Henry Moon (father):

Residence - 2 Montpelier Hill - December 9, 1887

Occupation - Private, 4th Royal Irish Dragoon Guards - December 9, 1887

- Henry Moon & Margaret Unknown
  - ○ Jane Moon – bapt. 11 Feb 1695 (Baptism, **St. Peter Parish**)
  - ○ Henry Moon – bapt. 26 Dec 1697 (Marriage, **St. Peter Parish**)

Henry Moon (father):

Residence - White Friar Lane - February 11, 1695

December 26, 1697

Hurst

- Henry Moon & Mary Unknown

  - Henry Moon – bapt. 10 Feb 1824 (Baptism, **St. Mary, Pro Cathedral Parish (RC)**)

Henry Moon (father):

Residence - Coombe - February 10, 1824

- Henry Moon & Unknown

  - John Moon – bapt. 13 Nov 1700 (Baptism, **St. Catherine Parish**)

  - Mary Moon – bur. 12 Jun 1714 (Burial, **St. John Parish**)

- James Moon & Catherine Fay – 20 Jan 1833 (Marriage, **St. Mary, Pro Cathedral Parish (RC)**)

- James Moon & Catherine Linard – 17 Aug 1817 (Marriage, **St. James Parish**)

- James Moon & Margaret Unknown

  - Michael Moon – bapt. 21 Sep 1742 (Baptism, **St. Catherine Parish (RC)**)

  - Honor Moon – bapt. 8 Jul 1744 (Baptism, **St. Catherine Parish (RC)**)

  - Margaret Moon – bapt. 12 Jul 1747 (Baptism, **St. Catherine Parish (RC)**)

  - William Moon – bapt. 8 Oct 1752 (Baptism, **St. Catherine Parish (RC)**)

- James Moon & Mary Unknown

  - Julie Moon – bapt. 11 Jul 1837 (Baptism, **St. Mary, Pro Cathedral Parish (RC)**)

- James Moon & Mary Anne Walsh

  - Richard Joseph Moon – b. 12 May 1872, bapt. 20 May 1872 (Baptism, **St. Agatha Parish (RC)**)

James Moon (father):

Residence - Spring Garden - May 20, 1872

- John Moon & Anne Moon

  - Catherine Moon – b. 30 Jun 1851, bapt. 21 Mar 1852 (Baptism, **St. Audoen Parish**)

Moon Surname Ireland: 1600s to 1900s

John Moon (father):

   Residence - 42 Back Lane - March 21, 1852

   Occupation - Tailor - March 21, 1852

- John Moon & Bridget Cosker

   o   John Moon – bapt. 30 Nov 1840 (Baptism, **St. James Parish** (RC))

- John Moon & Elizabeth Unknown

   o   Judith Moon – bapt. 29 Oct 1677 (Baptism, **St. Peter Parish**)

   o   Samuel Moon – bapt. 9 May 1681 (Baptism, **St. Peter Parish**)

- John Moon & Elizabeth Unknown

   o   Henry Moon – bapt. 1 Jul 1745 (Baptism, **St. Michan Parish** (RC))

   o   Mary Moon – bapt. 24 Aug 1746 (Baptism, **St. Michan Parish** (RC))

   o   Henry Moon – bapt. 20 Nov 1748 (Baptism, **St. Michan Parish** (RC))

- John Moon & Julie Kilbride

   o   Joseph Moon – b. 2 Dec 1858, bapt. 13 Dec 1858 (Baptism, **St. James Parish** (RC))

John Moon (father):

   Residence - Richmond Barracks - December 13, 1858

- John Moon & Mary Byrne (B y r n e)

   o   James Moon – bapt. 25 Apr 1831 (Baptism, **St. Nicholas Parish** (RC))

- John Moon & Mary Carey

   o   John Moon – b. 22 Mar 1858, bapt. 22 Mar 1858 (Baptism, **St. James Parish** (RC))

John Moon (father):

   Residence - 14 Bow Lane - March 22, 1858

Hurst

- John Moon & Mary Finn

  o John Moon – bapt. 7 Mar 1840 (Baptism, **St. Michan Parish (RC)**)

- John Moon & Mary Keeffe

  o William Moon – bapt. 13 Nov 1833 (Baptism, **Kinsale Parish (RC)**)

John Moon (father):

Residence - B Miles - November 13, 1833

- John Moon & Mary Unknown

  o Helen Moon – bapt. 19 Jun 1797 (Baptism, **St. Audoen Parish (RC)**)

- John Moon & Ruby Isabel Moon

Signatures:

  o Ethel Marguerite Moon & Percy Sumner Ewing – 26 Apr 1900 (Marriage, **St. George Parish**)

Signatures:

Ethel Marguerite Moon (daughter):

Residence - B Cowper Road - April 26, 1900

Moon Surname Ireland: 1600s to 1900s

Percy Sumner Ewing, son of Charles Henry Ewing & Eva A. Ewing (son-in-law):

    Residence - Alpha House, Drumcondra - April 26, 1900

    Occupation - Commercial Clerk - April 26, 1900

Charles Henry Ewing (father):

    Occupation - Traveller

John Moon (father):

    Occupation - Accountant

Wedding Witnesses:

John Moon, Ruby Isabel Moon, Charles Henry Ewing, & Eva A. Ewing

Signatures:

- John Moon & Sarah Moon
  - o John James Moon – b. 19 Apr 1858, bapt. 2 Jan 1859 (Baptism, **St. George Parish**)

John Moon (father):

    Residence - 3 Besborough Cottages, Royal Canal - January 2, 1859

    Occupation - Mechanist - January 2, 1859

Hurst

- John Moon & Unknown

    o   Dorcas Moon – bapt. 20 May 1710 (Baptism, **St. Nicholas Within Parish**)

- Joseph Moon & Alice Doyle

    o   Joseph Moon – b. 3 Jul 1872, bapt. 26 Jul 1872 (Baptism, **St. Agatha Parish (RC)**)

Joseph Moon (father):

Residence - 37 William Street - July 26, 1872

- Lawrence Moon & Dorothy Brien

    o   Mary Moon – bapt. 7 Oct 1827 (Baptism, **St. Catherine Parish (RC)**)

- Maurice Moon & Lucy Lacey – 22 Sep 1828 (Marriage, **St. James Parish**)

Maurice Moon (husband):

Residence - St. James Parish - September 22, 1828

Occupation - Sergeant, 17ᵗʰ Regiment - September 22, 1828

Lucy Lacy (wife):

Residence - St. James Parish - September 22, 1828

- Michael Moon & Elizabeth Cunningham

    o   Mary Moon – bapt. 15 Jul 1807 (Baptism, **St. Catherine Parish (RC)**)

- Michael Moon & Jane Smyth

    o   Elizabeth Moon – b. 1892, bapt. 1892 (Baptism, **St. Andrew Parish (RC)**)

Michael Moon (father):

Residence - 13 Stephen's Place - 1892

Moon Surname Ireland: 1600s to 1900s

- Michael Moon & Margaret Unknown

  o Mary Moon – bapt. 10 Mar 1765 (Baptism, **St. James Parish** (RC))

- Michael Moon & Mary Fitzsimmons – 17 Dec 1784 (Marriage, **St. Audoen Parish**)

Wedding Witnesses:

Margaret Moon & Sarah Domikin

- Nicholas Moon & Elizabeth McMahon – 15 Aug 1873 (Marriage, **Ballyferriter Parish** (RC))

- Patrick Moon & Bridget McNally

  o John Joseph Moon – b. 16 Apr 1865, bapt. 24 Apr 1865 (Baptism, **St. Michan Parish** (RC))

Patrick Moon (father):

Residence - 80 Lower Dorset Street - April 24, 1865

- Patrick Moon & Mary Kelly

  o Patrick Thomas Moon – b. 15 Oct 1878, bapt. 23 Oct 1878 (Baptism, **St. Mary, Pro Cathedral Parish** (RC))

Patrick Moon (father):

Residence - 19 Grenville Street - October 23, 1878

- Patrick Moon & Mary Mack

  o Michael Moon – bapt. 1819 (Baptism, **St. Mary Parish** (RC))

- Patrick Moon & Sarah Unknown

  o Bridget Moon – bapt. 1780 (Baptism, **St. Andrew Parish** (RC))

Hurst

- Peter Moon & Sarah Finlay

  o Sarah Moon – b. 27 Oct 1893, bapt. 27 Oct 1893 (Baptism, **St. Mary, Pro Cathedral Parish (RC)**)

Peter Moon (father):

Residence - 8 Gloucester Street - October 27, 1893

- Richard Moon & Alice Moon, bur. 24 Jan 1685 (Burial, **St. Michan Parish**)

Richard Moon (husband):

Occupation - Gentleman

- Richard Moon & Anne Unknown

  o Elizabeth Moon – bapt. 31 Jan 1821 (Baptism, **St. Mary, Pro Cathedral Parish** (RC))

Richard Moon (father):

Residence - King Street L H - January 31, 1821

- Richard Moon & Catherine Flood

  o Bridget Moon – b. 9 Jun 1862, bapt. 12 Jun 1862 (Baptism, **St. James Parish** (RC))

Richard Moon (father):

Residence - Richmond - June 12, 1862

- Richard Moon & Elizabeth Evans – Unclear (Marriage, **St. Peter Parish**)

Richard Moon (husband):

Occupation - Private - unclear

Moon Surname Ireland: 1600s to 1900s

- Richard Moon & Margaret Unknown

  o Anne Moon – bapt. 18 Jun 1838 (Baptism, **St. James Parish** (RC))

- Richard Moon & Mary Unknown

  o Olive Gertrude Moon – b. 8 Dec 1881, bapt. 22 Jan 1882 (Baptism, **Tralee Parish**)

Richard Moon (father):

Residence - Tralee - January 22, 1882

Occupation - Sergeant, 80ᵗʰ Regiment - January 22, 1882

- Silvestor Moon & Julie Hanlon

  o Elizabeth Moon – bapt. 4 Aug 1834 (Baptism, **St. Michan Parish** (RC))

- Terence Moon & Anne Unknown

  o Mary Moon – bapt. 14 Aug 1743 (Baptism, **St. Mary, Pro Cathedral Parish** (RC))

  o Thomas Moon – bapt. 23 Dec 1745 (Baptism, **St. Mary, Pro Cathedral Parish** (RC))

  o Anne Moon – bapt. 1 Apr 1747 (Baptism, **St. Mary, Pro Cathedral Parish** (RC))

  o Elizabeth Moon – bapt. 23 Jul 1750 (Baptism, **St. Mary, Pro Cathedral Parish** (RC))

  o Charles Moon – bapt. 1 Sep 1753 (Baptism, **St. Mary, Pro Cathedral Parish** (RC))

- Terence Charles Moon & Anne Carty – 23 Jun 1828 (Marriage, **St. Michan Parish** (RC))

  o George Moon – bapt. 20 Dec 1840 (Baptism, **St. Michan Parish** (RC))

- Thomas Moon & Anne Unknown

  o James Moon – bapt. 1774 (Baptism, **St. Andrew Parish** (RC))

- Thomas Moon & Anne Unknown

  o George Moon – bapt. 15 Jun 1832 (Baptism, **St. Michan Parish** (RC))

- Thomas Moon & Eleanor Moon

  o Anne Moon – bapt. 31 Dec 1815 (Baptism, **Aghold Parish**)

- Thomas Moon & Mary Keegan

  o Mary Moon – bapt. 6 Jun 1832 (Baptism, **St. Michan Parish (RC)**)

- Thomas Moon & Mary Tighe

  o Thomas Valentine Moon – b. 15 Feb 1891, bapt. 18 Feb 1891 (Baptism, **St. Mary, Pro Cathedral Parish (RC)**)

Thomas Moon (father):

Residence - 50 Tyrone Street - February 18, 1891

- Unknown Moon & Unknown

  o M. Moon

Signature:

- Unknown Moon & Unknown

  o Richard Weston Moon

Signature:

- William Moon & Elizabeth Moon

  o Elizabeth Moon – b. 28 Jun 1850, bapt. 9 Jul 1850 (Baptism, **Clontarf Parish**)

Moon Surname Ireland: 1600s to 1900s

William Moon (father):

    Residence - Clontarf - July 9, 1850

    Occupation - Workman - July 9, 1850

- William Moon & Elizabeth Moon

  o William Henry Moon – b. 1 Oct 1856, bapt. 21 Nov 1856 (Baptism, **St. Mark Parish**)

William Moon (father):

    Residence - 30 Lincoln Place - November 21, 1856

    Occupation - College Porter - November 21, 1856

- William Moon & Emily Anderson

  o Emily Moon & Patrick Fitzgerald – 15 Apr 1888 (Marriage, **Harrington Street Parish** (RC))

Emily Moon (daughter):

    Residence - 39 Daniel Street - April 15, 1888

Patrick Fitzgerald, son of John Fitzgerald & Mary McDonald (son-in-law):

    Residence - 10 Davis Street - April 15, 1888

- William Moon & Isabel Gannon

  o Ellen Mary Rosaline Moon – b. 25 Feb 1880, bapt. 29 Feb 1880 (Baptism, **St. Lawrence Parish**

  (RC))

William Moon (father):

    Residence - 21 Mager Street - February 29, 1880

- William Moon & Unknown

  o Mary Moon & James Garrett – 19 Jan 1888 (Marriage, **St. Peter Parish**)

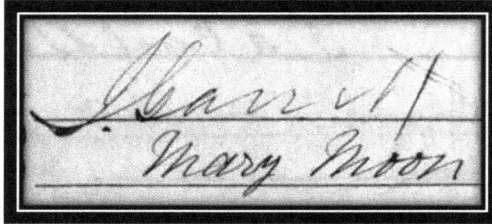

Signatures:

Mary Moon, daughter of William Moon (daughter-in-law):

Residence - 21 York Street - January 19, 1888

Coolderrry House, Carrickmacross - January 19, 1888

James Garrett, son of Robert Garrett (son-in-law):

Residence - Milltown Park, Shinrone, King's County - January 19, 1888

Occupation - Land Steward - January 19, 1888

Robert Garrett (father):

Occupation - Land Agent

William Moon (father):

Occupation - Land Steward

Wedding Witnesses:

Edward Rogers & Emily Rogers

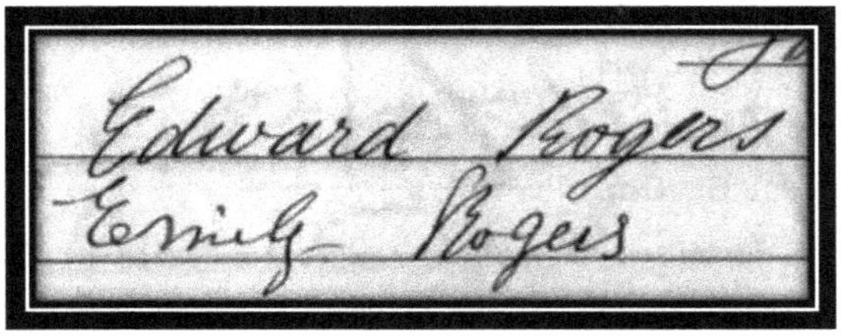

Signatures:

Individual Baptisms/Births

- Abraham Moon – b. 13 Dec 1763 (Baptism, **St. Paul Parish**)

- Bridget Moon – bapt. 25 Jul 1731 (Baptism, **St. Paul Parish**)

- Catherine Moon – bapt. 3 Sep 1738 (Baptism, **St. Paul Parish**)

- Hannah Moon – b. 16 Jul 1764 (Baptism, **St. Paul Parish**)

- Mary Moon – b. 5 May 1765 (Baptism, **St. Paul Parish**)

- Miller Moon – b. 1 Nov 1761 (Baptism, **St. Paul Parish**)

Individual Burials

- Alexander Moon – b. 12 Sep 1736 (Baptism, **St. Paul Parish**), bur. 18 Nov 1744 (Burial, **St. Paul Parish**)

- Anne Moon – b. 1833, bur. 12 Feb 1837 (Burial, **St. Peter Parish**)

Anne Moon (deceased):

  Residence - Kevin Street - before February 12, 1837

  Age at Death - 4 years

  Place of Burial - St. Kevin's Cemetery

- Catherine Moon – bur. 10 Dec 1749 (Burial, **St. John Parish**)

- Eleanor Moon – bur. 7 May 1723 (Burial, **St. Catherine Parish**)

- Eleanor Moon – bur. 9 Feb 1739 (Burial, **St. Paul Parish**)

Eleanor Moon (deceased):

  Age at Death - child

- James Moon – bur. 17 Mar 1729 (Burial, **St. Catherine Parish**)

- James Moon – bur. 29 Jun 1782 (Burial, **St. James Parish**)

James Moon (deceased):

  Residence - Watling Street - before June 29, 1782

Hurst

- John Moon – bur. 13 Sep 1676 (Burial, **St. Peter Parish**)

- John Moon – bur. 14 Feb 1677 (Burial, **St. John Parish**)

- John Moon – bur. 28 Jun 1701 (Burial, **St. Nicholas Without Parish**)

John Moon (deceased):

  Residence - Francis Street - before June 28, 1701

- John Moon – bur. 28 Dec 1762 (Burial, **St. James Parish**)

John Moon (deceased):

  Residence - Charles Street - before December 28, 1762

- Joseph Moon – bur. 7 Jun 1798 (Burial, **St. James Parish**)

Joseph Moon (deceased):

  Residence - Cooke Street - before June 7, 1798

- Margaret Moon – bur. 23 Feb 1728 (Burial, **St. Paul Parish**)
- Margaret Moon – bur. 14 Dec 1811 (Burial, **St. Peter Parish**)

Margaret Moon (deceased):

  Residence - New Street - before December 14, 1811

  Place of Burial - St. Kevin's Cemetery

- Mary Moon – bur. 22 Oct 1702 (Burial, **St. Catherine Parish**)
- Mary Moon – bur. 27 Oct 1702 (Burial, **St. Catherine Parish**)

Moon Surname Ireland: 1600s to 1900s

- Mary Moon – bur. 15 Mar 1717 (Burial, **St. Mary Parish**)

Mary Moon (deceased):

  Social Status - poor

- Mary Moon – bur. 14 Apr 1736 (Burial, **St. Nicholas Without Parish**)

Mary Moon (deceased):

  Residence - New Street - before April 14, 1736

- Mary Moon – bur. 15 Feb 1803 (Burial, **Glasnevin Parish**)

Mary Moon (deceased):

  Residence - Clarendon Street - before February 15, 1803

- Patrick Moon – b. 1832, bur. 26 Jan 1835 (Burial, **St. Peter Parish**)

Patrick Moon (deceased):

  Residence - Kevin Street - before January 26, 1835

  Age at Death - 3 years

  Place of Burial - St. Kevin's Cemetery

- Unknown Moon – bur. 17 Mar 1701 (Burial, **St. Peter Parish**)

Unknown Moon (deceased):

  Residence - King's Street - before March 17, 1701

Hurst

- Unknown Moon – bur. 1 Aug 1745 (Burial, **St. Nicholas Without Parish**)

Unknown Moon (deceased):

Residence - Patrick Street - before August 1, 1745

- Unknown Moon – bur. 18 Jun 1758 (Burial, **St. John Parish**)
- Unknown Moon – bur. 30 May 1784 (Burial, **St. Nicholas Without Parish**)

Unknown Moon (deceased):

Residence - Hanover Lane - before May 30, 1784

- Unknown Moon – b. 1797, bur. 4 Oct 1815 (Burial, **St. Audoen Parish**)

Unknown Moon (deceased):

Residence - St. Thomas Parish - before October 4, 1815

Age at Death - 18 years

- William Moon – bur. 11 Jun 1786 (Burial, **St. John Parish**)
- William Moon – bur. 9 May 1803 (Burial, **St. Paul Parish**)
- William Moon – b. Mar 1864, bur. 2 Aug 1864 (Burial, **Taney Parish**)

William Moon (deceased):

Residence - Rosemount - before August 2, 1864

Age at Death - 5 months

Individual Marriages

- Anne Moon & Matthew Kelly

  o Frances Kelly – bapt. 1 Dec 1840 (Baptism, **St. Michan Parish** (RC))

- Anne Moon & Michael Ennis

  o Mary Anne Ennis – b. 3 Apr 1870, bapt. 4 Apr 1870 (Baptism, **SS. Michael & John Parish** (RC))

  o Michael Patrick Ennis – b. 30 May 1875, bapt. 7 Jun 1875 (Baptism, **SS. Michael & John Parish** (RC))

Michael Ennis (father):

Residence - 79 Cook Street - April 4, 1870

45 George's Street - June 7, 1875

- Anne Moon & Patrick Larkin

  o Julie Larkin – bapt. 26 Dec 1830 (Baptism, **SS. Michael & John Parish** (RC))

- Anne Moon & Philip Gurley

  o Philip Gurley – b. 4 Mar 1870, bapt. 10 Mar 1870 (Baptism, **SS. Michael & John Parish** (RC))

Philip Gurley (father):

Residence - 3 Lower Exchange Street - March 10, 1870

Hurst

- Bridget Moon & Edward Hughes

  o Catherine Mary Hughes – b. 1884, bapt. 1884 (Baptism, **St. Andrew Parish** (RC))

Edward Hughes (father):

Residence - 10 Creighton Street - 1884

- Bridget Moon & John Noonan

  o John Noonan – b. 1894, bapt. 1894 (Baptism, **St. Andrew Parish** (RC))

John Noonan (father):

Residence - 23 Lower Erne Street - 1894

- Catherine Moon & Benjamin Campbell

  o Mary Anne Campbell – b. 4 Aug 1869, bapt. 10 Sep 1869 (Baptism, **St. Nicholas Parish** (RC))

Benjamin Campbell (father):

Residence - 31 New Row - September 10, 1869

- Catherine Moon & Daniel Sullivan

  o Margaret Sullivan – bapt. 7 Aug 1833 (Baptism, **Kinsale Parish** (RC))

Daniel Moon (father):

Residence - Francis Street - August 7, 1833

- Catherine Moon & Dennis Coakly

  o Dennis Coakly – bapt. 6 Mar 1833 (Baptism, **Clonakilty Parish** (RC))

Dennis Coakly (father):

Residence - Miles - March 6, 1833

Moon Surname Ireland: 1600s to 1900s

- Catherine Moon & James McStoker – 13 May 1823 (Marriage, **St. James Parish**)

- Catherine Moon & Richard Watkins – 3 Nov 1872 (Marriage, **Cork - South Parish** (RC))

Wedding Witnesses:

Pierce Moon & Rachel Aherne

- Elizabeth Moon & Patrick Tierney (T i e r n e y) – 14 Jan 1833 (Marriage, **St. Michan Parish** (RC))

- Ellen Moon & Dennis Cleary

  - Daniel Cleary – bapt. 5 Jan 1834 (Baptism, **Clonakilty Parish** (RC))

Dennis Cleary (father):

Residence - Garanishil - January 5, 1834

- Ellen Moon & John Leary

  - Margaret Leary – bapt. 9 Feb 1834 (Baptism, **Clonakilty Parish** (RC))

John Leary (father):

Residence - Desart - February 9, 1834

- Ellen Moon & Matthew Daly

  - Matthew Daly – bapt. 26 May 1859 (Baptism, **Caharagh Parish** (RC))

Matthew Daly (father):

Residence - Killeenloagh - May 26, 1859

- Jane Moon & Leonard Shortel – 19 Jul 1719 (Marriage, **St. Catherine Parish**)

Hurst

- Julie Moon & Maurice Griffin

  - Peter Griffin – b. 5 Jul 1842, bapt. 5 Jul 1842 (Baptism, **Abbeydorney Parish (RC)**)

Maurice Griffin (father):

Residence - Ballavin - July 5, 1842

- Margaret Moon & Bartholomew Linehan

  - Mary Linehan – bapt. 5 Sep 1833 (Baptism, **Kinsale Parish (RC)**)

Bartholomew Linehan (father):

Residence - [Hard to Read] Quay - September 5, 1833

- Margaret Moon & Matthew Heyland – 24 Jun 1773 (Marriage, **St. Catherine Parish (RC)**)

Wedding Witnesses:

William Heyland & Mary Mecum

- Mary Moon & Daniel McCarthy

  - Ellen McCarthy – bapt. 18 Apr 1834 (Baptism, **Clonakilty Parish (RC)**)

Daniel McCarthy (father):

Residence - B Nurchir - April 18, 1834

- Mary Moon & Edward Maher

  - Edward James Maher – b. 1882, bapt. 1882 (Baptism, **St. Andrew Parish (RC)**)

Edward Maher (father):

Residence - 15 Lower Erne Street - 1882

Moon Surname Ireland: 1600s to 1900s

- Mary Moon & Edward Medicot

  - James Edward Medicot – bapt. 19 Jul 1807 (Baptism, **St. Michan Parish** (RC))

- Mary Moon & John Lee

  - Mary Lee – bapt. 1773 (Baptism, **SS. Michael & John Parish** (RC))

- Mary Moon & Joseph Irwin

  - Unknown Irwin – b. 1 Sep 1864, bapt. 9 Sep 1864 (Baptism, **St. Nicholas Parish** (RC))

Joseph Irwin (father):

Residence - 26 Cuff Street - September 9, 1864

- Mary Moon & Robert Cording

  - Edwin Edward Cording – b. 1871, bapt. 1898 (Baptism, **Chapelizod Parish** (RC))

Robert Cording (father):

Residence - Blackhorse Lane, Devonshire - 1898

- Mary Moon & Patrick Griffin

  - Catherine Griffin – b. 20 Oct 1813, bapt. 20 Oct 1813 (Baptism, **Ballyferriter Parish** (RC))

Patrick Griffin (father):

Residence - Bulinabuck - October 20, 1813

- Mary Anne Moon & David Thermer (T h e r m e r) Thompson – 26 Mar 1819 (Marriage, **St. Paul Parish**)

- Mary Anne Moon & Thomas Curry

  - Patrick Curry – b. 1884, bapt. 1884 (Baptism, **St. Andrew Parish** (RC))

Thomas Curry (father):

Residence - 2 Rock Lane - 1884

Hurst

- Sarah Moon & Bryan Brisland

  o James Brisland – bapt. 15 Oct 1839 (Baptism, **Rossalettiri & Kilkeraunmor (Roscarbery & Lissevard) Parish (RC)**)

Bryan Brisland (father):

Residence - Milkcove - October 15, 1839

- Sarah Moon & Bernard (B e r n a r d) Ward

  o Margaret Ward – bapt. 6 Jun 1784 (Baptism, **St. Nicholas Parish (RC)**)

Moon Surname Ireland: 1600s to 1900s

Name Variations

Includes Latin and Abbreviated forms of names found in the original documents.

Abigail = Abigale, Abigall

Anne = Ann, Anna, Annae

Bartholomew = Barth, Bartholmeus, Bartholomeo

Bridget = Birgis, Brigid, Brigida, Bridgit

Catherine = Catharine, Catharina, Catharinae, Catherina, Cath, Catha, Cathae, Cathe, Cathn, Kate

Charles = Carolus, Charls, Chas

Christopher = Christoph

Daniel = Danielem, Danielis

Edmund = Edmond

Edward = Ed, Edwd

Eleanor = Eleo, Eleonora, Elinor, Ellenor

Elizabeth = Betty, Elisa, Elisabeth, Eliz, Eliza, Elizab, Elizh, Elizth

Ellen = Elena, Ellena

Emily = Emilia

Esther = Essie, Ester

Francis = Fransicum

George = Geo, Georg, Georgius

Grace = Gratiae

Gulielmo = Guil, Guillelmi, Gulielmum, Guillelmus, Gulmi

Helen = Helena

Moon Surname Ireland: 1600s to 1900s

Honor = Hanora, Honora

James = Jacobi, Jacobus, Jas

Jane = Joanna

Jeanne = Jeannae, Joannae

Joan = Johanna, Joney

John = Jno, Joannem, Joannes, Johannis

Joseph = Jos

Juliana = Julian

Leticia = Letitia, Lettice, Letticia

Lewis = Louis

Luke = Lucas

Margaret = Margarita, Margaritae, Margeret, Marget, Margt

Martha = Marthae

Mary = Maria, My

Mary Anne = Marianna, Marianne, Maryanne

Michael = Michaelis, Michl

Patrick = Pat, Patt, Patk, Patricii, Patricius

Peter = Petri

Richard = Ricardi, Ricardus, Rich, Richd

Robert = Roberti

Rose = Rosa, Rosae

Thomas = Thom, Thomae, Thoms, Thos, Ths

Timothy = Timotheus, Timy

William = Wil, Will, Willm, Wm

Notes

Notes

Notes

Notes

Notes

Notes

Index

M

Hurst

Hanes
1766 Feb 23 3
Hannah
1835 Sep 15 4
Helen
1797 Jun 19 8
Henry
1697 Dec 26 5
1745 Jul 1 7
1748 Nov 20 7
1824 Feb 10 6
Honor
1744 Jul 8 6
James
1774 13
1782 4
1831 Apr 25 7
Jane
1695 Feb 11 5
John
1700 Nov 13 6
1777 Nov 6 1
1778 4
1788 Oct 20 4
1840 Mar 7 8
1840 Nov 30 7
1858 Mar 22 7
John James
1859 Jan 2 9
John Joseph
1865 Apr 24 11
Joseph
1783 4
1844 Feb 24 3
1858 Dec 13 7
1872 Jul 26 10
Judith
1677 Oct 29 7
Julie
1837 Jul 11 6
Lily Elizabeth
1887 Dec 9 5
Mabel Louise
1888 Mar 7 2

Margaret
1747 Jul 12 6
1878 Jul 30 1
Mary
1706 4
1743 Aug 14 13
1746 Aug 24 7
1765 Mar 10 11
1777 4
1794 4
1807 Jul 15 10
1826 2
1827 Oct 7 10
1832 Jun 6 14
Mary Jane
1859 Aug 22 4
Michael
1742 Sep 21 6
1819 11
Olive Gertrude
1882 Jan 22 13
Patrick Michael
1862 Jan 31 5
Patrick Thomas
1878 Oct 23 11
Peter
1790 Jun 29 4
Richard
1701 May 10 3
Richard Joseph
1872 May 20 6
Samuel
1681 May 9 7
Sarah
1893 Oct 27 12
Terence
1776 May 19 2
Thomas
1745 Dec 23 13
Thomas Valentine
1891 Feb 18 14
Unknown
1857 May 6 4
William

Hurst

T

U

About The Author

Donovan Hurst graduated from San Diego State University with a Bachelor of Arts in the major field of studies of History and a minor in the field of studies of Anthropology. He is a current member of The General Society of Mayflower Descendants and has been conducting genealogical research for over 10 years tracing back his ancestors to their ancestral homelands in Denmark, England, France, Germany, Ireland, Norway, and Scotland.

www.ingramcontent.com/pod-product-compliance
Lightning Source LLC
Chambersburg PA
CBHW081203270326
41930CB00014B/3275